MANAGING YOUR TIME

MANAGING YOUR TIME

LOTHAR J SEIWERT

KOGAN PAGE

There is also an audio cassette based on this book.
ISBN 0-7494-1094-9
Available from Kogan Page, address below. Telephone 071-278 0433.

Copyright © Gabal e V 1989

All rights reserved. No reproduction, copy or transmission
of this publication may be made without written permission.

No paragraph of this publication may be reproduced, copied
or transmitted save with written permission or in accordance
with the provisions of the Copyright Act 1956 (as amended),
or under the terms of any licence permitting limited copying
issued by the Copyright Licensing Agency, 7 Ridgmount Street,
London WC1E 7AE.

Any person who does any unauthorised act in relation to
this publication may be liable to criminal prosecution and
civil claims for damages.

Most of the cartoons are by Erik Liebermann and are
reproduced by permission.

First published in the Federal Republic of Germany 1984,
revised edition 1989. Other foreign language editions:
Dutch 1988; Esperanto 1989; Finnish 1986; French 1987; Greek 1989;
Hungarian 1989; Russian 1989; Spanish 1989; Swedish 1989

First published in Great Britain in 1989 by
Kogan Page Limited, 120 Pentonville Road,
London N1 9JN.

Reprinted 1990, 1991, 1992, 1994

British Library Cataloguing in Publication Data

A CIP catalogue record for this book is available from
the British Library

ISBN 0-7494-0056-0
ISBN 1-85091-952-6 *pbk*

Typeset by DP Photosetting, Aylesbury, Bucks
Printed and bound in Great Britain by
Biddles Limited, Guildford and King's Lynn

◀ CONTENTS ▶

1. Use Your Time Properly	7
2. Catch the Time Thieves	13
3. Define Your Goals	17
4. Make Your Plans in Writing	23
5. Use Daily Schedules	27
6. Set Priorities	33
7. Start With a Positive Attitude	39
8. Watch the Performance Curve	43
9. Reserve Quiet Time for Yourself	49
10. Manage by Delegation	53

11. Use a Time Planner 59

12. Try to be Consistent 65

Further Reading 71

USE YOUR TIME PROPERLY

'Very few people have enough time and yet almost everyone has all the time in the world.'

Time is the most valuable resource we have. In some languages, it is the most frequently used noun. Time is more valuable than **money**. Our time capital must be invested carefully. We could describe our lives as the time allotted to us here on earth. Our most important task in **life** is to make the most of this time.

Time is valuable **capital**:

- Time is a finite, scarce commodity.
- Time cannot be bought.
- Time cannot be saved up or stored.
- It is impossible to increase time.
- The passage of time is constant and irrevocable.
- Time is life.

We cannot stop the passage of time.

- How much is one hour of time in your life worth to you?

- Are you as careful with your time as you are with your money?

Time is
- money

- life

- capital

Take stock of yourself

7

MANAGING YOUR TIME

We cannot stop the passage of time.

Time capital is scarce

Our limited **time capital** can only be estimated: a person with a high life expectancy has available to him or her a maximum of 200,000 hours of time. Treat today as the first day of the rest of your life.

Use your time!

Realisation of potential only 30-40 per cent

The degree to which human performance potential is realised in the business sector is estimated to be a mere 30 to 40 per cent. In other words, it is reckoned that most people waste at least 60 per cent of their working time. Most time and energy are wasted because of a lack of clear objectives, planning, priorities and perspective.

With which of the following statements do you agree?

USE YOUR TIME PROPERLY

True False

- Many success-orientated and career-orientated members of the workforce complain of being pressed for time and being **overloaded with work** (the overtime syndrome). □ □ **Overtime**

- Many frequently feel **stressed**. It is often necessary to deal with several things simultaneously. Heavy responsibilities and a heavy workload, frequent tight deadlines, a multitude of tasks and other responsibilities result in time pressure and stress. □ □ **Stress**

- Many people are not in control of their work, but **are controlled by it**. A frequent problem is that you merely react instead of taking the initiative. Customers, your boss, your colleagues, telephone calls and a variety of tasks constantly occupy you around the clock with the result that although you are always busy, you make little real progress. □ □ **Reactive instead of proactive**

- Many managers do not get down to their real work until after hours. They cannot find time to do it during the day because there are too many **distractions**. These distractions, such as protracted meetings, decide the order of the day, and managers are frequently sidetracked by matters of secondary importance. □ □ **Distractions**

- Studies have shown that, for many of these people, the most important problem is the **conflict between work and leisure time**. Time dedicated to their profession and to working overtime cannot be spent with the family, and, as might be expected, becomes a cause for frustration. □ □ **Insufficient leisure time**

A better **use** of this valuable and limited time can only be attained through conscious, continuous and consistent time management: **Use of time**

Managing your time means being in control of your time and work, rather than allowing them to control you. **Time management**

All truly **successful people** have one thing in common: at some point **Approach**

9

MANAGING YOUR TIME

Be master of your own time!

in their lives they sat down and did some **hard thinking** about the possible uses and rewards to be gained from their personal **time capital**.

Goals   Life can only be wholly successful if it is based on a well-considered time concept or **life concept**: we must make a conscious effort to use the time available to us to attain our professional and personal goals. This is the only way to establish a direct link between coping with daily tasks and activities on the one hand and ensuring personal satisfaction and progress on the other.

Success   What counts is not in which direction the wind is blowing, but rather how you set the sails! Successful **time management** shows you new ways to:

Perspective   • gain a better **perspective** of pending activities and priorities;

Creativity   • make more opportunities to be **creative** (taking the initiative instead of reacting);

USE YOUR TIME PROPERLY

- deal with, reduce and avoid **stress**; **Reduce stress**
- gain more **leisure time**, ie more time for family, friends and for yourself; **Leisure time**
- consistently and systematically attain your **goals**, so that your life takes on meaning and a sense of direction. **Goals in life**

Take time to ...

Take time to work; it is the price of success. **Take your time**
Take time to think; it is the source of power.
Take time to play; it is the secret of perpetual youth.
Take time to read; it is the fountain of wisdom.
Take time to be friendly; it is the road to happiness.
Take time to love; it is the joy of life.
Take time to laugh; it is the music of the soul.
  (Adapted from an old English prayer)

Starting today, how are you going to make better use of your time? **Plan of action**

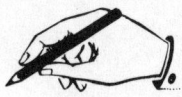

11

CATCH THE TIME THIEVES

'Part of our time is stolen from us, or else we are cheated out of it, and whatever is left over seems to disappear unnoticed.' (Seneca)

When things do not go as we had planned or expected, it is often because we are repeatedly **interrupted**. Sometimes it is our own fault, but sometimes others around us are responsible.

Interruptions

Surroundings

- Start with a **study of your own working habits**.

Self-analysis

Who or what is robbing us of time? Which **time thieves** can we identify? The following questions are intended to help you check your own personal work situation and identify the **distractions**.

- **Time thieves**
- **Distractions**

Self-assessment: my time thieves	*T*rue			
	almost always	fre- quently	some- times	almost never
1. The **telephone** constantly interrupts me and the conversations are usually longer than necessary.				
2. Numerous **visitors** from outside or within the company often keep me from carrying out my work.				

Telephone

Visitors

13

MANAGING YOUR TIME

	Self-assessment: my time thieves	*True*			
		almost always	fre- quently	some- times	almost never
Meetings	3. **Meetings** frequently last much too long, and the results are often unsatisfactory for me.				
'Procrastinitis'	4. Weighty tasks, ie time-intensive and thus often less pleasant, are usually put off, or else I have difficulty in following them through to their conclusion, since I never seem to have the necessary quiet (**procrastinitis**).				
Lack of priorities	5. I lack **priorities**, and I try to perform too many tasks at once. I spend too much time on trivial matters and can't seem to concentrate enough on the most important tasks.				
Deadline pressure	6. Often I can only meet my schedules and deadlines under **deadline pressure**, because something unexpected always comes up, or because I have taken on more than I can handle.				
Paperwork	7. There is too much **paperwork** on my desk; correspondence and reading take up too much time. My desk is not exactly a model of order and tidiness.				

CATCH THE TIME THIEVES

Self-assessment: my time thieves	*True*			
	almost always	fre-quently	some-times	almost never
8. There is frequently insufficient **communication** with others. Delayed exchanges of **information**, misunderstandings or even bad feelings are routine.					Communications and information
9. **Delegation** of tasks almost never works out, and often I have to take care of things that could be attended to by others.					Delegation
10. It is difficult for me to **say no** when others ask me to do something and I should actually be doing my own work.					Saying no
11. I don't have any clear professional or personal **objectives**, ie it is often difficult for me to see the real meaning of what I am doing all day and every day.					Objectives
12. Sometimes I lack the necessary **self-discipline** actually to carry out when I have resolved to do.					Self-discipline
Count the ticks you have made in each column and add up the total points. (Don't forget to multiply by the numbers given at the bottom of the columns.)	× 0	× 1	× 2	× 3
	= 0	+	+	+

TOTAL = ... points

MANAGING YOUR TIME

Solution

0–17 points:
You do not plan your time and you allow your schedule to be determined by others. You are not able to manage yourself, let alone others. **Time management** will mark the start of a new and successful life for you.

18–24 points:
You try to organise your time, but you are **not persistent** enough to be successful.

25–30 points:
Your time management is **good** – but it could be better.

31–36 points:
Congratulations (if you have been honest in your answers)! You are a **model** for anyone who would like to learn how best to manage his or her time. Let others benefit from your experience and pass on the ABCs of time management.

Plan of action

Starting today, what are you going to do to catch three of your time thieves?		
Time thieves	Causes, reasons	Possible solutions

 DEFINE YOUR GOALS

'Having lost sight of our goal, we redoubled our efforts.'
(Mark Twain)

Successful management is only possible given clear, well-defined objectives and subsequent monitoring to check that the objectives have been attained. **Objectives** are a challenge for all participants and stimulate **action**: you know where you want to go and what **final result** you want to achieve. At the same time, these objectives set **standards** for evaluating performance. **Management by objectives** is both an efficient and an amenable method used in corporate and staff management.

Objectives
Action
Final result
Standards
Management

MANAGING YOUR TIME

Objectives as a life concept

Not only successful companies but also successful individuals have firm **objectives**. Success in life must be based on a well-considered **life concept**, ie clear objectives for one's career and private life that are purposefully striven for. This is the only way to establish a direct link between **today's** various **tasks** and **tomorrow's success** and satisfaction.

Today's tasks Tomorrow's success

Perspective Priorities Abilities

Only a person who has defined his or her objectives can retain a proper **perspective** in the hectic pace of everyday life. Even under a heavy workload, he or she establishes correct **priorities** and knows how to make optimum use of his or her **abilities** in order to reach the desired objectives quickly and confidently. This applies both to professional life and to leisure time and family life.

Activate the subconscious

A person who has, and pursues, conscious objectives, also directs his or her **subconscious powers** towards his or her activities through self-motivation and self-discipline. Having objectives helps to **focus your powers** on the real points at issue. It is not so much a question of **what you do** but rather **why you do it**. Setting objectives is a necessary prerequisite and is the key to successful **time management**.

Time management

20 per cent of the time spent produces 80 per cent of the results

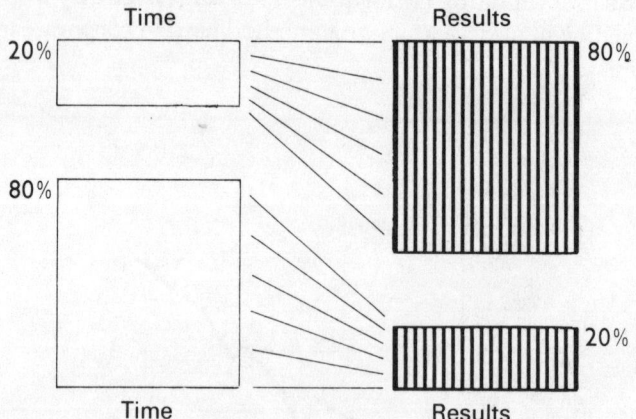

80:20 Rule (Pareto's law)

DEFINE YOUR GOALS

But where should you begin? Many people spend most of their time dealing with numerous relatively **minor problems** and tasks instead of concentrating on a few **essential activities**. However, as little as 20 per cent of time and effort used efficiently will produce the following results:

- 20 per cent of **customers** or goods account for 80 per cent of **turnover**.
- 20 per cent of production **errors** cause 80 per cent of product **rejects**.
- 20 per cent of a **newspaper** contains 80 per cent of the **news**.
- 20 per cent of **meeting time** produces 80 per cent of the **decisions**.
- 20 per cent of **desk work** makes possible 80 per cent of the **success in one's work**.

Discrepancy between minor and essential activities

This correlation of the **80:20 Rule** was first described by the Italian economist Vilfredo Pareto in the nineteenth century. Using statistical studies, Pareto found that 20 per cent of the population owned 80 per cent of the national wealth. This state of affairs, which is also known as **Pareto's law**, could also be applied to many other spheres of activity.

The 80:20 Rule

Pareto's law

As far as setting objectives and planning action to reach those objectives are concerned, the **20:80 success factors** in one's professional and private life must be identified and given top priority.

Setting objectives: priority for 20:80 per cent success factors

Plan of action

> Starting today, what are you going to do to bring the planning of your daily activities more into line with your objectives or strategic success factors (in accordance with the **80:20 Rule**)?
>
> _____
> _____
> _____
> _____

19

- Which objectives do you wish to achieve?
- Be clear about your objectives and make a list of **all the professional and personal objectives** you wish to attain in the near or distant future.

Which professional objectives do you wish to achieve?	
My career objectives	Active steps to reach objectives
_____	•
_____	•
_____	•
_____	•
My professional objectives	Active steps to reach objectives
_____	•
_____	•
_____	•
_____	•
_____	•
_____	•
_____	•
My job objectives	Principal tasks demanded by my job
_____	•
_____	•
_____	•
_____	•

DEFINE YOUR GOALS

Which personal objectives do you wish to achieve?

My objectives in life	Active steps to reach objectives
_____	•
_____	•
_____	•
_____	•

What do you want to be or do?	Steps to reach objectives
_____	•
_____	•
_____	•
_____	•
_____	•
_____	•
_____	•
_____	•

Other personal objectives (experiences I would like to have; things I would still like to do, etc)

_____ •

_____ •

_____ •

_____ •

MAKE YOUR PLANS IN WRITING

'He who sows not in spring, shall not reap in autumn.'
(Proverb)

The better we organise our time (ie plan), the better we can use our time for attaining our personal and professional objectives. Planning means preparation for the realisation of objectives. The main advantage of planning your work is:

Plan your time to achieve your objectives

Planning means saving time

Experience in business shows that the more effort dedicated to time planning, the less time is necessary for execution, and time is saved in the long run:

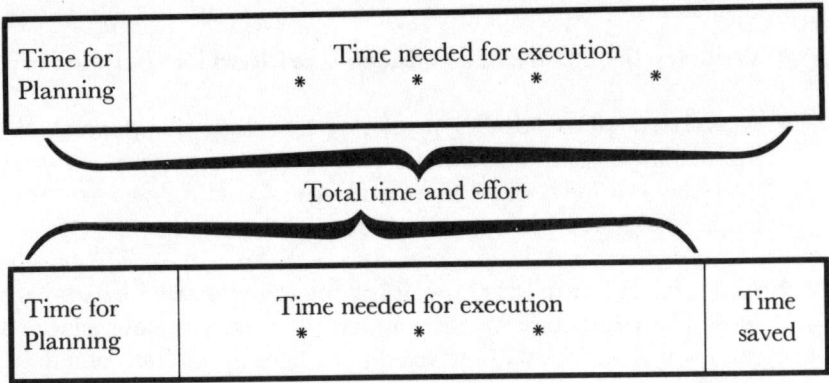

* = Time investment necessary for trouble-shooting

23

MANAGING YOUR TIME

8 minutes' planning = 1 hour of time saved

Eight minutes of preparation for each working day and consistent follow-through based on this planning can result in an additional **one hour** per day for more essential things.

Advantages of time planning

What are the advantages of planning your time?	True/ False
Reaching goals • Professional and personal objectives are reached more quickly and more confidently.	
Saving time • Time is saved and can be spent on really important tasks and objectives (management, colleagues, thinking, family, leisure time).	
Keeping track • You have time to keep track of all projects, tasks and activities.	
Reducing stress • The stress of daily life is reduced, and you have a more predictable daily routine.	

Principle of putting things in writing

The most important rule in planning is to **put things in writing**.

- **Controlling schedules**
- Schedules of which you have 'only made a mental note' are harder to **control** ('out of sight, out of mind'), and it is easy to stray from them.

- **Reduction in workload**
- Written schedules mean a **reduced workload** for your memory.

- **Self-motivation**
- A **written plan** has the psychological effect of inducing self-motivation in your work. Your activities when carrying out your everyday routine become more goal-orientated, and you are more inclined to adhere to the set tasks for the day.

- **Concentration**
- As a result, you are less easily distracted (**concentration**) and are more likely to persist in carrying out the tasks you have planned than you would be without fixed guidelines in the form of a daily schedule.

MAKE YOUR PLANS IN WRITING

- By checking daily results, you keep track of tasks not yet carried out (which should be transferred to another day).
- **Checking**

- Furthermore, you can increase your success by establishing better estimates of your time needs and of distractions, and by allowing for more realistic buffer times for unforeseen events.
- **Success**

- Written schedules, kept in a separate folder, provide automatic documentation of the work which you have performed, and in certain cases can serve as evidence and a record of your activities – or of your inactivity (or inability to act).
- **Documentation**

Apart from your own inertia, what is stopping you from writing a list of the tasks you wish to carry out?

_____

_____

Plan of action

Do you have no time to do this? If so read the following story about the saw:

A hiker, strolling through a wood, met a lumberjack frantically and laboriously sawing a fallen tree trunk into smaller pieces. The hiker approached the lumberjack to see why he was struggling so hard with his work, and then commented: 'Excuse me, but I couldn't help noticing

MANAGING YOUR TIME

that your saw is completely blunt! Wouldn't it be better to sharpen it?' Completely out of breath, the lumberjack groaned: 'I don't have time – I have to get this sawing finished!'

When do you intend to sharpen *your* saw?

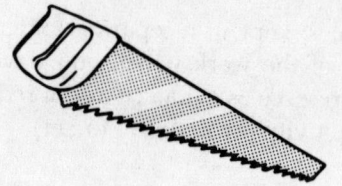

USE DAILY SCHEDULES

'The more exactly you plan, the harder you are hit by chance.'
(Managerial proverb)

When you begin to work with time schedules, it is important, first of all, to **plan each** individual **day**:

Begin with daily planning

- The **day is the smallest and most manageable unit** in systematic time scheduling.
- If the previous day was not successful, one can **begin each day anew**.
- If you do not have your **daily work routines** under control by means of planning, it will be impossible to maintain plans for longer periods, such as the month or the year.

- Manageable unit
- You can always start again
- Preliminary stage for long-term planning

A **realistic daily schedule** should contain only what you wish, or have, to **take care of that day** – and also what you are able to handle! Indeed, the more you consider the set goals to be attainable, the more you will mobilise yourself to reach them.

Daily schedule
=
Daily objectives

The **LEADS method** is relatively simple and requires an average of only eight minutes of planning time per day to gain **more time for the essentials**:

LEADS method

27

MANAGING YOUR TIME

List activities
Estimate time needed
Allow time for unscheduled tasks
Decide on priorities
Scan scheduled tasks at end of day.

1. List important tasks

List your tasks, activities and deadlines

Using a Daily Schedule form, list everything you wish to, or must, accomplish on the day in question under the appropriate headings.

- Tasks
- Unfinished and
- unexpected matters
- Deadlines
- Communication
- Regular events

- Make a **checklist of jobs to be done** and the deadlines for this week or month, see activities checklist, page 56
- List **unfinished business** from the previous day
- **New work** for the day

- **Deadlines** to be met
- **Telephone calls and correspondence** to be taken care of
- **Regular activities**, eg departmental meeting from 2 to 3 pm.

2. Estimate the time needed

Estimate the time your tasks will take

Note the approximate time you must allocate for each of your tasks.

Be careful not to overplan

Time is scarce. Eight hours are only eight hours. Experience shows that the amount that can be achieved within a certain time is often overestimated, and more activities are planned that can actually be performed.

This results in unnecessary frustration and a dislike of daily schedules.

Calculate time spent as you would money spent

For this reason, make a rough **estimate** of **the time** that your planned activities require. Time is more important than money. When you **spend money**, you make a rough estimate of how much an article will cost, if not an exact calculation. Why not do the same with your time capital?

Set time limits

Another rule borne out by experience states that the time available to perform a task often determines how much time is required to perform

USE DAILY SCHEDULES

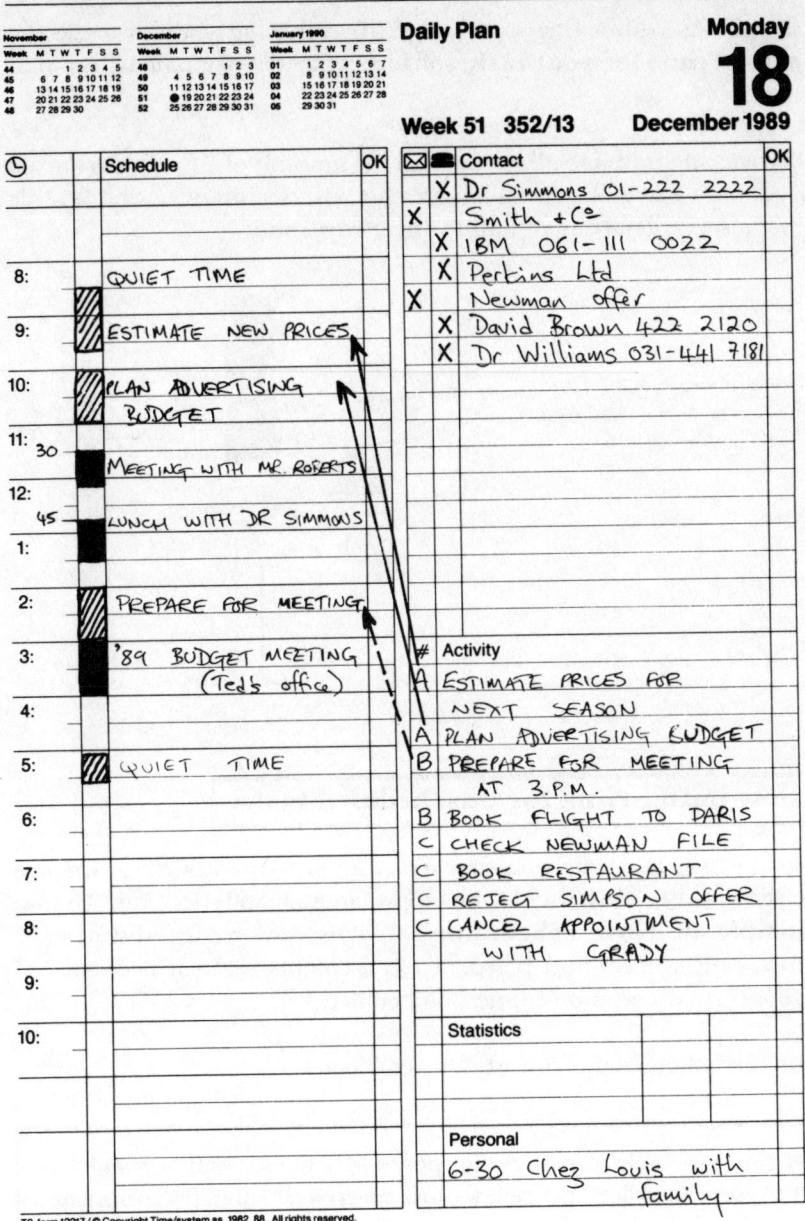

MANAGING YOUR TIME

that task. As with a financial budget, by allowing yourself a specific amount of **time for your task**, you force yourself to remain within that limit.

Eliminate interruptions

Moreover, if you have allotted a specific amount of time to perform a certain task, you will work in a more concentrated manner, and be able to call a more determined halt to **interruptions**.

Since he's been working under pressure of time, he seems to be only a shadow of his former self.

3. Allow buffer time

The basic principle of time scheduling: schedule only 60 per cent

Allow buffer time for unscheduled tasks

Schedule only a certain proportion of your working hours; experience has shown that this should be approximately 60 per cent (**basic principle of time scheduling**). Unforeseen events, disturbance factors, time thieves and personal requirements make it necessary to leave a certain amount of time unscheduled.

Your time plan should consist of three blocks:

Time planning: three blocks

- Approximately 60 per cent for **planned** activities (daily schedule)
- Approximately 20 per cent for **unexpected** activities (interruptions, time thieves)
- Approximately 20 per cent for **spontaneous** and **social** activities (creative time).

USE DAILY SCHEDULES

If you wish to be prudent, it may even be advisable to plan only 50 per cent of working time, and to reserve the other 50 per cent as buffer time.

Principle of prudence: plan only 50 per cent

Decide on priorities, be selective, delegate

Since there is a tendency to plan more than 50 to 60 per cent of available working time, you must rigorously cut down your list of tasks to realistic proportions by:

- setting priorities
- being more selective
- and delegating.

The remainder will have to be postponed, cancelled or handled in overtime.

4. Prioritise your tasks – limit your daily amount of work

Reduce list of tasks to realistic proportions

- **Priorities**
- **Selection**
- **Delegation**

- **Remainder**

Scan scheduled tasks at the end of the day
Putting off unfulfilled tasks

Whenever you have **repeatedly postponed a task**, it becomes a nuisance, and there are two options available to you:

- You can tackle this task at long last which means that it is then **taken care of**.
- You can cancel the task, because the matter has **taken care of itself**.

5. Scan schedule – monitor planned tasks

Convert postponement of tasks into positive action

Starting today, how are you going to prepare regular **daily schedules**?
_____
_____
_____
_____

Plan of action

Using the form on page 29, prepare your daily schedule for the next day.

SET PRIORITIES

'It is better to do the right work (= effectiveness) than to do the work "right" (= efficiency).'

(Peter Drucker)

Two major problems in management are the constant **temptation to do too much at once** and the risk of **dissipating energy** among individual tasks. At the end of a hard working day, you may realise that, although you have worked hard, **important matters have been left unattended** to or have not been completed.

Trying to do too much at one time

Important things are unfinished

Successful managers are characterised by their ability to handle numerous, as well as different, activities by devoting themselves to **one single task** at any one time. As a result, they are always dealing with one matter only, but doing this in a persistent and determined manner. This needs **clear priorities** and the ability to stick to them.

Work on one task at a time = clear priorities

Setting priorities means deciding which tasks have top priority, secondary priority, etc and which are to be handled as low priority. Tasks with **top priority** must be performed first.

Most important tasks (top priority) first

The advantages of setting priorities

By ranking your tasks in order of importance, you ensure that:

Advantages of setting priorities

MANAGING YOUR TIME

- Importance
- Urgency
- Concentration
- Time saved
- Objectives attained
- Delegation

- Daily results

- Increased performance

- you work on **important** tasks first;
- if necessary, you work on tasks according to their **urgency**;
- you **concentrate** on just one task at a time;
- you handle the tasks more **effectively** in the time scheduled;
- the set **objectives are attained** as effectively as possible under the circumstances;
- all tasks which can be performed by others are put aside and **delegated**;
- at the end of the **planned period** (eg, a working day), the most important matters are at any rate taken care of;
- the assignments by which you and your **achievements** are judged **are completed**.

The positive effects: **What do you wish to achieve?**	×
• Deadlines met • More satisfactory work flow and work results • Increased satisfaction among workers, colleagues and superiors • Avoidance of conflict • Your own satisfaction increased and you avoid unnecessary stress	

SET PRIORITIES

ABC analysis

A **value analysis of the use of time** shows that the relative proportions of actual time spent on **very important (A)**, **important (B)** and **less important (C)** tasks will vary, depending on the position of the person involved (eg a personnel director will differ in this respect from a finance director).

Actual time use does not correspond to the value of the activity

Value analysis of the use of time (ABC analysis)

	Value of the activity	
65%	20%	15%
A tasks	**B tasks**	**C tasks**
very important	important	trivial/routine
15%	20%	65%

Actual use of time

ABC analysis

- Concentrate on A tasks
- Delegate B tasks
- Get rid of C tasks

Time is frequently wasted on trivial problems (C), while the few essential tasks (A) are usually neglected. The key to successful time management is to give the scheduled activities a clear priority by ranking them according to an ABC classification scheme:

Concentrate on A tasks

Priorities: ABC

- **A tasks** are the most important tasks of management. They can be carried out properly only by the person involved or by a team (ie they cannot be delegated), and are of the utmost importance in fulfilling the managerial function in question.

A tasks very important; cannot be delegated

- **B tasks** are tasks of average importance and can be delegated.

B tasks important

- **C tasks** are tasks which are least important in fulfilling a function, but represent the largest share of work (routine tasks, paperwork,

C tasks less important

35

MANAGING YOUR TIME

reading, telephoning, files, correspondence and other administrative work).

Set priorities using ABC analysis

The ABC analysis certainly does not mean that only A tasks should be performed and C tasks may be dispensed with completely, but rather that all these activities should be brought into a balanced relationship with each other, given the correct rank, and organised into a daily work sequence by means of setting priorities.

A tasks are important tasks which cannot be delegated.

Practical application
- 1-2 A
- 2-3 B
- Rest C

In practice, ABC analysis functions best when you:

- schedule only one or two **A tasks** per day (approximately three hours);
- earmark a further two to three **B tasks** (approximately one hour);
- set some time for **C tasks** (approximately 45 minutes).

Take the initiative instead of just reacting
Goal-orientated instead of activity-orientated

In this way you **actively control your sequence of work**, concentrate on the **essentials** and avoid conflicts and unnecessary stress. However, many managers insist on doing things right (**activity-orientated**) instead of doing the right things (**goal-orientated**).

SET PRIORITIES

Once you have worked through your daily list you will find that you have time left over, despite disturbances and the unexpected; you can then reconsider in what way and for what purpose you wish to use this extra time.

What are the A tasks for the assignment you are currently performing?
- _____
- _____
- _____
- _____
- _____

Starting today, how are you going to ensure that you work on at least one A task each day?
_____
_____

What are you going to do with the time gained from consistently setting priorities and carrying them through?
_____
_____

Plan of action

START WITH A POSITIVE ATTITUDE

'A merry heart maketh a cheerful countenance; but by sorrow of the heart the spirit is broken.'

(Proverbs, 15.13)

It's almost always the same problem: you **rush** to the office **without enough sleep** or a decent breakfast, pressed for time and in a tearing hurry. Just the kind of start that could easily make **your day go wrong**! In the morning, you should allow yourself time to:

- **wake up** peacefully;
- have a pleasant **breakfast** with your family;
- enjoy **washing** and getting dressed;
- **drive to work** at a leisurely and unhurried pace.

You should try to take pleasure in something positive each day, because our basic attitude towards our environment – that is, the attitude with which we approach the job in hand – contributes significantly to our success or failure. All the how-to-achieve success pundits unanimously agree that success depends very strongly on a person's attitude, thoughts, feelings and frame of mind, and that these can be influenced correspondingly by **positive thinking and positive action**.

A bad start means a bad day

A good start means a good day

Lead a positive life

The importance of a positive lifestyle

Positive thinking and positive action

MANAGING YOUR TIME

Each day, you should do something that you enjoy.

In order to keep a **positive attitude** each day, you should observe **three rules**:

Three positive rules

- Enjoyment
- Attaining objectives

- Leisure time

- Do something each day that you **enjoy**.
- Do something each day that brings you measurably closer to your personal **objectives**.
- Do something each day that **balances your private life with your professional life** (sport, family, hobbies, etc).

Before work

Before launching yourself into your **day's routine**, you should calmly prepare yourself by:

- Review the daily schedule

- **reviewing your daily schedule** (which you prepared the previous evening), keeping in mind your routine tasks and objectives for the day, and remembering their order of importance and urgency;

- Prepare A tasks

- carrying out the necessary **preparatory work** and assembling the documents you will need for the **priority tasks of the day** (A tasks).

Before going home

Before rushing out of your office at the end of the day, you should calmly bring your working day to a close and prepare yourself mentally for your journey home, the evening ahead and your leisure time by:

40

- making a **target-performance comparison of the daily schedule** with respect to your objectives;
- making a list of those **tasks which were not completed** and which will have to be **transferred to the next day**;
- **preparing the schedule for the next day**. Thus, during the evening and before going to bed, you will not be preoccupied with what tomorrow might have in store.
- **thinking positively** about the quality of your day and what you got out of it in terms of personal satisfaction;
- thinking about how you would like to spend the **evening**. Many people come home from work in the evening without having given any thought as to how to make others happy and how to spend **an enjoyable evening**.

- Check daily schedule
- Transfer unfinished tasks
- Plan for the next day
- Evaluate the day
- Put yourself in the right mood for the evening

'And how was *your* day?'

MANAGING YOUR TIME

Plan of action

Starting tomorrow, what are you going to do to start your day positively?
_____
_____
_____

What possibilities do you see for giving the evening a highspot (family, children, theatre, concert, a good book, friends, going out, sport, relaxation, etc)?
_____
_____
_____

WATCH THE PERFORMANCE CURVE

'The early bird catches the worm.'

(Proverb)

During the day, everybody's **performance potential** is subject to fluctuation. This fluctuation manifests itself in a natural rhythm which varies from person to person but is predictable in each case. Statistically measured, average daily performance and the way it fluctuates can be described using the following graph (standard curve of the REFA Work Study Association).

Rhythmic fluctuations in performance ability

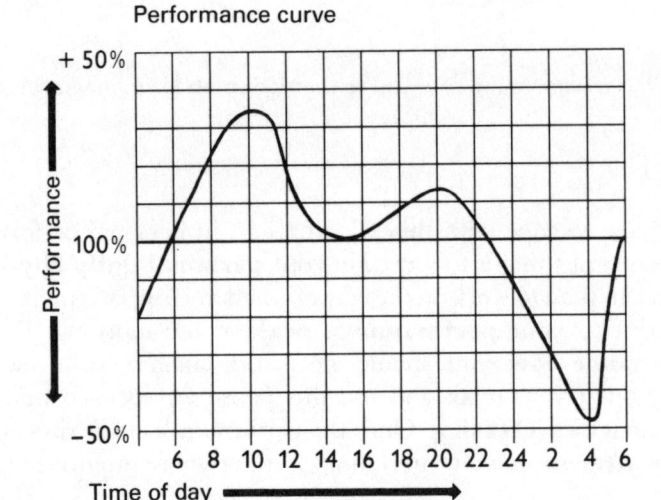

Performance curve

Physiological performance fitness as a percentage

43

MANAGING YOUR TIME

Individual differences – and common features

Maximum performance in the morning
Minimum performance after lunch
Second high early in the evening

Although there are a number of **differences** from person to person which are influenced by nutritional habits and other personal characteristics, the following basic statements can still be made:

- **The maximum performance level** usually occurs in the **morning**. This level is not reached again during the rest of the day.
- In the **afternoon**, the well-known **after-lunch** period of **inactivity** begins. Some people try to overcome it with large doses of strong coffee. This, however, usually prolongs its duration.
- After a **second high-performance phase in the evening**, the performance curve drops continuously until it reaches its lowest point a few hours after midnight.

'What makes you so sure you're the right man for management?'

Personal daily rhythm
- Performance high: A tasks
- Performance low: C tasks
- Second high: B tasks

We all have to cope with these fluctuations in personal performance. The important thing is to ascertain your **personal daily rhythm**, so that you can plan to work on the complicated and important matters (**A tasks**) during your **performance peak** in the morning. During a **performance low** you should not work against your biological rhythm, but try to relax and use this phase for social contacts and routine activities (**C tasks**). Once the performance curve rises again **in the late afternoon**, you can resume work on more important tasks (**B tasks**).

44

WATCH THE PERFORMANCE CURVE

Now draw your own personal performance curve:

Performance curve

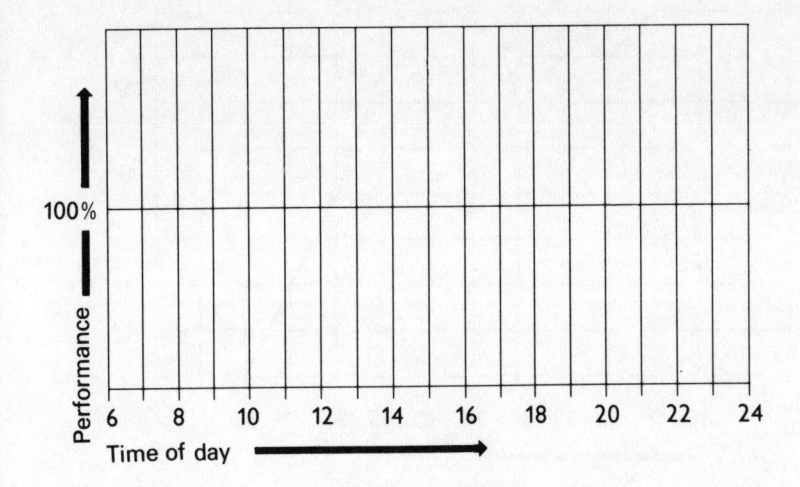

(Graph: Performance (%) vs Time of day, 100% marked on y-axis; x-axis from 6 to 24 in increments of 2)

If you take advantage of the **natural laws which govern your body's performance** by organising your day according to the **performance curve**, you will **increase your productivity** considerably without having to make major changes or resort to desperate measures.

Increased performance

A complicated, unpleasant task which demands concentration is much easier to deal with in the morning than during the low performance phase, when it will require a far greater effort.

A tasks

Working too long and too intensively is not worthwhile anyway, since concentration and performance ability diminish and mistakes appear. Don't consider **breaks** as a waste of time, but as a welcome opportunity to 'recharge your batteries'.

Breaks to recharge batteries

MANAGING YOUR TIME

Concentration performance values over a 60-minute period

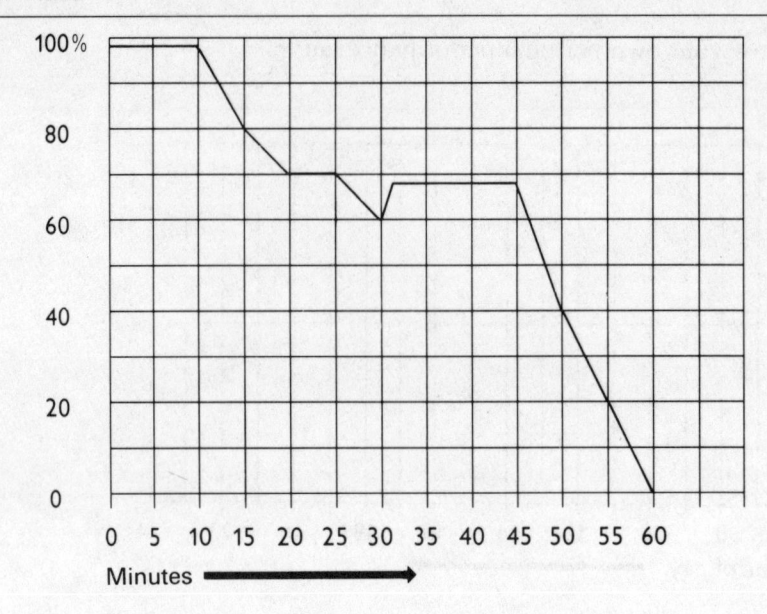

Optimal recuperative value: maximum 10-minute break after 1 hour of work
Regular short breaks

Medical studies have shown that the **optimum recuperative value** of breaks is realised after approximately one hour of work. The break should last 10 minutes at most, since the optimum effect is realised in the **first 10 minutes** and tends to diminish thereafter:

- Accordingly, your **daily schedule** should include **regular but brief breaks**.

46

WATCH THE PERFORMANCE CURVE

- You can considerably increase the regenerative effect of the breaks you take if you try to relax, get some exercise and fresh air.

Exercise
Fresh air

Starting today, what are you going to do to improve your daily performance by adapting your daily schedule to your biorhythm?
_____
_____
_____

Plan of action

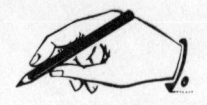

Starting today, what are you going to do to make the best use of the regenerative effect of short breaks?
_____
_____

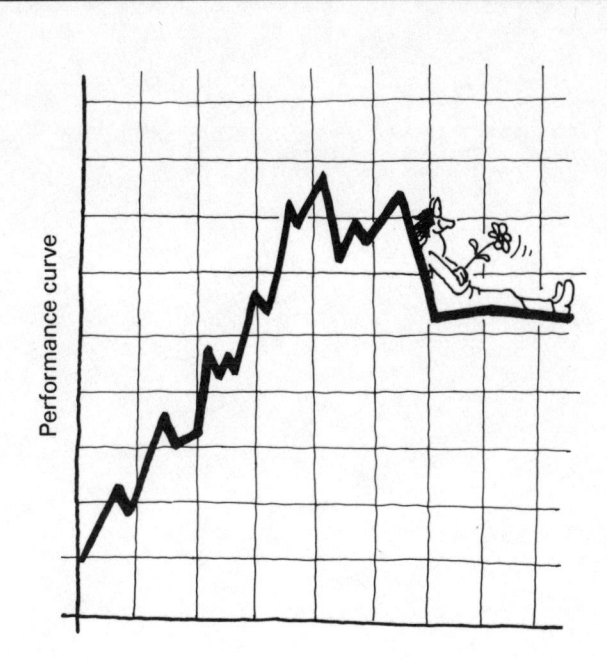

Performance curve

47

RESERVE QUIET TIME FOR YOURSELF

'The greatest events are not our loudest hours, but rather our most quiet.'

(Nietzsche)

Many managers start their 'real' work after **official office hours**. They don't have time for it during the day because there are too many **distractions**: colleagues, customers, unannounced visitors, disagreements, telephone calls, meetings, etc. It may be that a permanent **open door** is appreciated by everyone else, but the manager who allows his time to be invaded in this way is doing himself a disservice.

Overtime
Distractions
Open door

If someone is constantly disturbed or his work is interrupted, a '**saw-blade**' effect manifests itself; even if that person is distracted for only a moment, he or she will need additional time in order to get back into the work and continue where he or she left off. Added together, these performance losses can account for **up to 28 per cent of lost time**.

Saw-blade effect

Performance loss: 28 per cent time lost

MANAGING YOUR TIME

Reduction in performance capability as a result of work constantly interrupted

Time lost because of:
- **increasingly longer restart times**
- **constantly decreasing concentration**

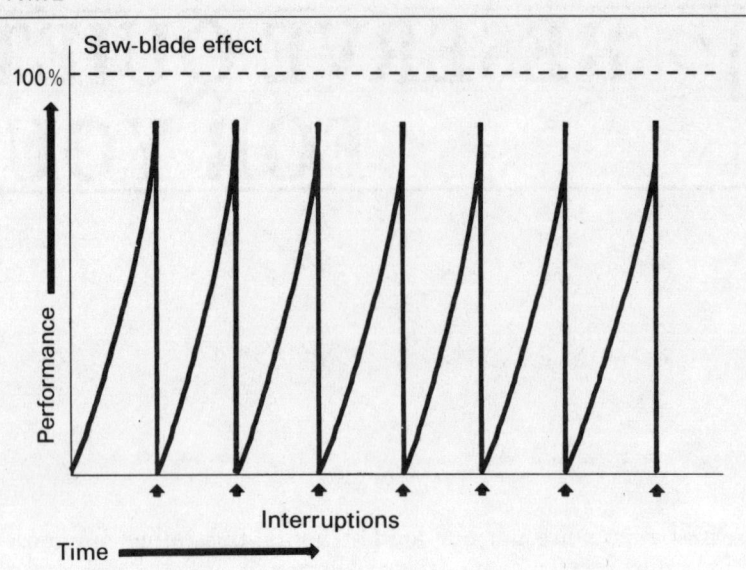

Saw-blade effect

100%

Performance

Interruptions

Time

1 hour of interruption-free time for A tasks

In order to perform the most important tasks (**A tasks**), it is essential to work with as **few interruptions** as possible. It is astonishing what you can achieve when allowed to work for **one hour** without being disturbed. But how can you put this into practice?

'Why can't you work in an office like other people?'

Quiet time
Undisturbed period

A system which has proved effective is to set up a **quiet time** or **'blocked' period** during which you are not to be disturbed.

RESERVE QUIET TIME FOR YOURSELF

If you are honest with yourself, you will have to admit that it is **not essential** to be **accessible** round the clock or always to be **personally available**. Business will go on as usual, even if you yourself are off for an hour (or more?). As a rule, you are not likely to be disturbed when you have an appointment with someone or when you attend a meeting. Therefore, consider these personal undisturbed times in the same way as an important appointment, or even as *the* most important appointment.

Don't always be available

Period of undisturbed time = Time saved

| **An appointment with yourself!** |
| **(QUIET TIME)** |

Appointment with yourself

In terms of **organisation**, you should handle quiet time as you would any other important appointment when you will be absent or unavailable:

Organise quiet time

- Note down your quiet time in your daily schedule as you would a meeting or a visit from a customer.

- **Daily schedule**

- Protect yourself during your quiet time (ideally, with the help of your secretary) - close the door to your office and, before doing so, tell your colleagues that you 'won't be there'.

- **Protect yourself**

'Ah, I thought I'd find you under "M", Mr McDonald.'

MANAGING YOUR TIME

Calling back

Incoming telephone calls or enquiries from colleagues, etc can be taken by your secretary, who can arrange for you to return calls and get back to people. This may seem standoffish, but at least once a day your important tasks should have absolute priority.

Blocked period
Distraction curve

When planning blocked periods, the low-disturbance and high-disturbance times of the day should be taken into account. The daily distraction curve shows this pattern for a typical day in the office:

Daily distruption curve
- Low-disturbance times
- High-disturbance times

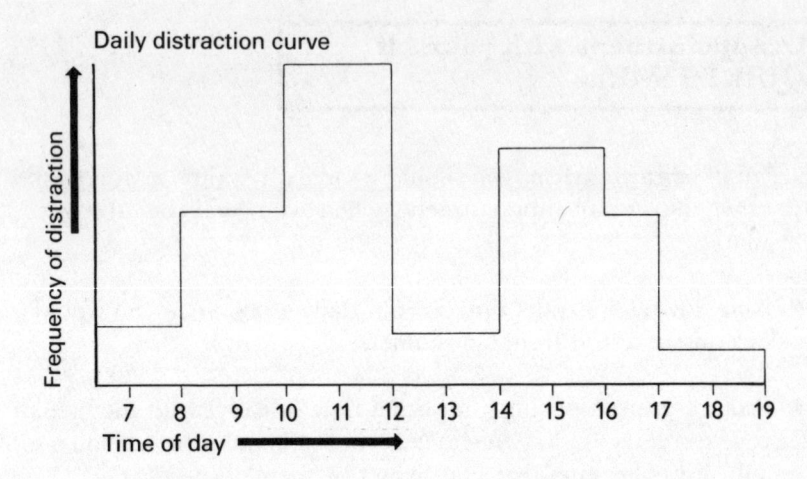

Daily distraction curve

(graph: Frequency of distraction vs Time of day, 7 to 19)

Organise your day

You should try to work in accordance with the distraction curve by:

Quiet time: A tasks

- scheduling your quiet time for working on your most important tasks (A tasks) during those times when you are less likely to be disturbed;

High-disturbance time: C tasks

- expecting more frequent interruptions and carrying out less important tasks (C tasks) at times when you are more likely to be disturbed.

Plan of action

Starting today, what are you going to do in order to enjoy quiet time on a regular basis?

_____
_____
_____

MANAGE BY DELEGATION

'The person doing the work loses the overall picture.'
(Croatian proverb)

Delegation is the key activity of every employee and of every manager. Delegating brings considerable direct and indirect benefits.

Management *is* delegation

MANAGING YOUR TIME

	With which of the arguments in favour of delegation do you agree?	Yes/No
• **Time saved**	• Delegating **eases the strain** on management and creates **time for important tasks** (eg for actual management functions).	
• **Employees' abilities**	• Delegating helps to exploit the **specialised knowledge and experience of the employees** involved.	
• **Employee development**	• Delegating helps to **promote and develop** the abilities, initiative, self-reliance and competence of **employees**.	
• **Employee motivation**	• Delegating often has a positive effect on the **motivation** and **job satisfaction of employees**.	

Have you said yes to several, or even all, of these points? If so, you will agree with our hypothesis:

Delegation: advantages for management and staff

> Delegating is equally advantageous for management *and* employees; it means:
>
> - **reducing one's own workload** and providing **time for A tasks**; and it
> - provides **employees** with an opportunity for **development** (**motivation**).

Transfer of authority and responsibility

As a rule, delegation – when used correctly – will meet with mainly positive reactions from employees. Correct delegation in this sense means the **transfer of tasks and authority as well as of responsibility**.

Successful delegation
- **Willingness**
- **Ability**

Successful delegation requires two things:

- a willingness to delegate;
- the ability to delegate.

MANAGE BY DELEGATION

If you are not delegating effectively, you are also not organising your time effectively. Willingness involves a personal decision on your part. With respect to ability, here is a summary of the most important rules for delegating a task successfully:

Check the '**Rules for Delegation**' (quick analysis).

Delegation checklist

- **What** needs to be done? (details)
- **Who** should do it? (individual members of staff)
- **Why** should this member of staff do it? (motivation, objective)
- **How** should the member of staff do it? (scope, details)
- **When** should it be completed? (deadline)

- What?
- Who?
- Why?
- How?
- When?

Rely more on 'management by delegation'!

Management by delegation

- Look at each task again; is it absolutely necessary that you carry out this activity yourself, or is it just as feasible (or even more feasible) for the task to be performed by a colleague?

  ● **Colleagues' abilities**

- While maintaining a certain level of supervision, you should also delegate medium-term and long-term tasks in your area of responsibility. This will motivate your staff and expand their knowledge and ability.

  ● **Medium- and long-term tasks**

- As far as the work and the abilities of your staff permit, **delegate as often and as much as possible each day**.

  ● **Each day**

- Delegate not only to your staff, but also to other departments and to internal and external **service units**.

  ● **Service units**

MANAGING YOUR TIME

Activities Checklist/Task Monitor

- Effective delegation requires a well-organised work situation: task delegation should also be planned, and you should monitor the delegated tasks and deadlines using an '**Activities Checklist/Task Monitor**'.

Activities Checklist/Task Monitor

May

Date	Priority A	Priority B	Priority C	Activity/Task	Delegated to	Start	Finish by
2/5	X			FINISH T/S ADVERTISING CONCEPT	MYSELF		30/5
3/5		X		PREP. HET PLANNING CONF.	H. MILLER	5/5	20/5
3/5		X		DRAFT IHK PRESENTATION	SALES DEPT		18/5
5/5		X		CHECK ABSENTEEISM REPORT	MYSELF		10/5
7/5			X	CONVENE IBM PROJECT GROUP	TOM HAYDEN		16/5
7/5			X	WRITE DATA PROCESSING ARTICLE	MYSELF		30/5
8/5			X	ORGANISE BMW FACTORY TOUR	Jean Smith		16/5
17/5			X	COMPILE SALES REPORT	BILL ROGERS		21/5
12/5			X	SUBMIT SEMINAR SCHEDULE	MYSELF		30/5

Quick decisions

Delegating according to the Eisenhower grid

Establishing priorities

The decision grid is a simple, practical **delegation** tool which dates back to Dwight **Eisenhower**, the American general and president. It is particularly useful when a **quick decision** must be made as to which tasks should receive priority. **Priority** is assigned according to the criteria of

- **urgency** and **importance**.

Depending on whether the task is of greater or lesser importance or **urgency**, there are four possibilities for evaluating and (subsequently) carrying out tasks:

Eisenhower principle

B tasks Fix a deadline (or delegate at once)	**A tasks** Tackle immediately
P	**C tasks** Delegate

Axes: Importance (vertical), Urgency (horizontal)

Quick analysis based on
- Importance
- Urgency

In terms of **practical application**, this means that:

- You must personally see to tasks which are both **urgent** and **important**. They should be tackled immediately (**A tasks**).

- Tasks which are very important but not yet urgent can wait for the time being, but should be **planned**, ie given a schedule or **delegated** under supervision (**B tasks**).

- Tasks which are not very important but which are urgent should be **delegated** or tackled in **order of decreasing importance (C tasks)**.

- You should distance yourself from tasks which are less urgent as well as less important (**bin** or **file**).

Be a little more daring when it comes to **taking risks** and opt for the **wastepaper basket** more often. Things frequently take care of themselves if they lie around long enough!

Practical application
- Take care of A tasks immediately
- Schedule, delegate B tasks
- Delegate C tasks in decreasing order of importance
- Waste bin, file

Take risks: use your waste bin more!

MANAGING YOUR TIME

Plan of action

What is stopping you from delegating more tasks, starting today?
_____
_____
_____

What can you delegate today/tomorrow from your checklist?
_____
_____
_____

USE A TIME PLANNER

'It is not enough to come to the river intending to fish. You also have to bring a net.'

(Old Chinese proverb)

Successful managers are also successful at managing their time. They have succeeded in bringing their activities under control so as to give them **more time for the essentials**. The secret of success for many employees and managers is the daily use of a personal work aid, which allows them to:

- Keep an **overall picture** of all tasks at hand;
- **plan** and coordinate all **important projects**, appointments and activities in a systematic and goal-orientated way; and
- be more successful in organising and **monitoring** the execution and follow-up of these tasks.

A **time planner** is the best tool for setting up, organising and maintaining self-discipline. This may take many forms, some commercially available. However, a time planner is **much more than an appointment diary**. As a rule, an appointment diary is simply a memory aid for appointments and dates, and does not contain a list of activities, priorities, deadlines and set objectives for tasks that you wish to handle personally or delegate.

Successful time management

- *Overall picture*
- *Planning*
- *Monitoring*

Time planner

More than an appointment book

MANAGING YOUR TIME

Successful managers are also successful at managing their time.

Ring-binder
Loose-leaf
Many functions

- A time planner usually consists of a practical ring-binder system with loose-leaf pages, and can thus be supplemented at any time by the addition of new pages. It is an appointment calendar, journal, notebook, planning tool, memory aid, address book, reference work, catalogue of ideas, telephone directory and a monitoring tool all rolled into one. As your constant personal companion, it also functions as a written memory, a mobile office and a miniature databank.

- **Memory aid, schedules, forms**

- The **time planner** is the most important practical element in a consistent time-planning system. It is your personal memory aid for all **schedules**, **forms** and **checklists** used in your working day.

- **Principle of putting things in writing**

- The **time planner** ensures successful personal goal planning and time scheduling and better use of your valuable time. It implements the time-planning principle of **putting things in writing**. You have a constant and complete **overall picture** of all agreements, plans and major projects, and you can react quickly to changing situations.

USE A TIME PLANNER

- Depending on the particular type you use, a **time planner** generally contains the following:

- a **diary** section with a calendar spreadsheet for the year and planning forms, for example, for daily schedules, with reminders for subsequent months and weeks, etc;

- a **professional and personal data section** with forms, pages for notes, lists and information; for example, for project planning, trade fair appointments, turnover figures, postal charges, book lists, flight connections, hotel addresses, income and expenses, tax deadlines, blank pages, an ideas file, checklists, etc;

- a section for noting **addresses and telephone numbers**

- **a general section** with transparent covers and separate compartments for cheques, stamps, credit cards, company ID cards, banknotes, photos etc.

Side notes: Format, functions • Diary section • Data section • Addresses, telephone numbers • Miscellaneous

Which is more efficient: an appointments diary or a time planner?

A simple appointments diary can never fulfil the functions of a time planner. A comparison shows the decisive advantages of using a time planner:

- When **coordinating appointments**, your personal **planning, monitoring and controlling aid** always accompanies you.

- It is organised so that **information is always easily accessible** – when travelling, during visits to customers, at meetings, in the office or at home.

- Your **checklists** and other **planning and decision-making** aids are **always available**.

- Essential data and information can be kept at hand for **direct access** in a very **compact** form.

Side notes: Performance comparison: appointment diary v time planner
- Aid always with you
- Information always easily accessible
- Decision-making aids always available
- Direct access to data

61

MANAGING YOUR TIME

- **Versatile ring-binder**
- You can expand, supplement or remove parts from your **ring binder** at any time.

Time saved is money saved

10 per cent improved efficiency through management by time planner = one hour of time saved each day

Conventional appointments diaries, which are used for noting appointments only, **spell trouble for successful time management**. Using a **time planner** enables you to improve the planning, organisation, coordination and efficiency of your daily work. The time planner improves the quality and success of your own work. The manufacturers often promise 15 to 40 per cent more available time, but about only **10 per cent improved efficiency** translates into **one full hour** of time saved each day through effective **time planning management**!

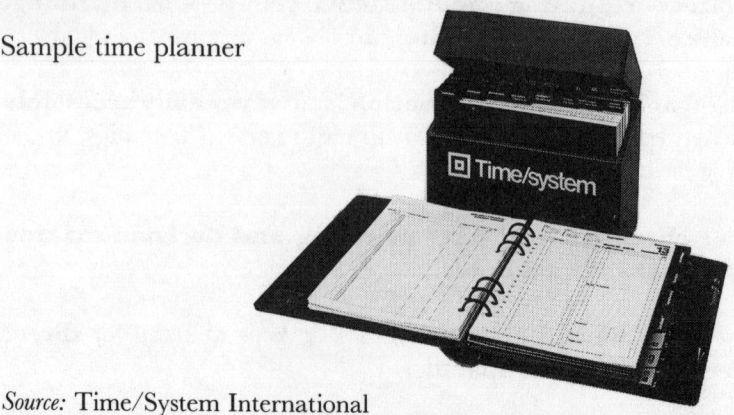

Sample time planner

Source: Time/System International

USE A TIME PLANNER

Use a time planner – it is the most important work tool for **managing your time**.

What advantages does a time planner have over its diary-type predecessors which you have used up to now?

_____
_____
_____

Starting today, what can you do to improve the organisation of your daily routine using a time planner?

_____
_____
_____

Plan of action

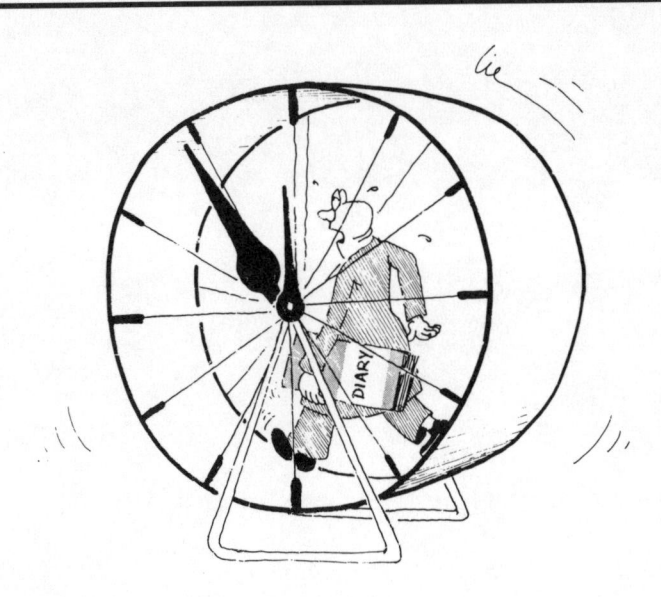

63

TRY TO BE CONSISTENT

'All things are difficult before they become easy.'

(Persian proverb)

MANAGING YOUR TIME

Consistent time management has many advantages:

Advantages and benefits of time management

▶ What do you wish to achieve?	×
• Better preparation for the next working day • A plan of the day ahead • A clear overall picture of daily objectives • Organisation of your daily routine • Better memory	
• Concentration on the essentials • Less dissipated energy • Achievement of daily objectives • Differentiation between important and less important matters • Decisions on priorities and delegation	
• Increased efficiency through coordination of tasks • Reduction of distractions and better handling of interruptions • Self-discipline • Reduced stress and nervous strain • Composure in the face of unforeseen events	
• Improved self-control • Positive sense of achievement at the end of the day • Increased satisfaction and motivation • Increase in personal performance potential • And, above all, time saved through working methodically (quiet time)	

Time management = Time saved

To re-emphasise the last and perhaps the most important aspect:

! Successful application of time-planning techniques and work methods can save you between 10 and 20 per cent of your time every day.

Summary

The following chart illustrates the most important principles:

TRY TO BE CONSISTENT

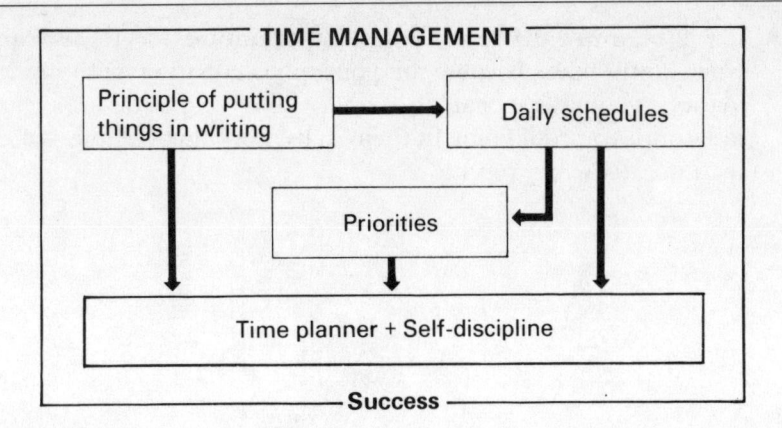

```
┌──────────── TIME MANAGEMENT ────────────┐
│                                          │
│  ┌─────────────────┐      ┌────────────┐ │
│  │ Principle of    │ ───▶ │ Daily      │ │
│  │ putting things  │      │ schedules  │ │
│  │ in writing      │      └────────────┘ │
│  └─────────────────┘            │        │
│         │      ┌───────────┐    │        │
│         │      │ Priorities │◀──┘        │
│         │      └───────────┘             │
│         │            │                   │
│         ▼            ▼                   │
│  ┌─────────────────────────────────────┐ │
│  │ Time planner + Self-discipline      │ │
│  └─────────────────────────────────────┘ │
└──────────── Success ─────────────────────┘
```

Consistently managing your time on the principles described in this book will not only lead to improved clarity of perception, scheduling and monitoring, but will also reduce stress, and thus contribute to a positive, optimistic attitude to life.

Consistent time management – positive attitude to life

This can be achieved by amazingly simple means and a minimum of time and effort, requiring approximately **8 minutes a day**.

8 minutes a day

At the end of each day, become accustomed to planning your next working day in writing. Visualise the sequence of **events on the following day**.

Plan the next day the evening before

Consider which tasks are **most important** and must be taken care of on the next day, and **write down** a time by which you intend to get them done.

Put your tasks in writing

The **psychological background**:

Psychological background

- On your way home or on the way to the office in the morning, your **subconscious** will already have started working on these tasks and be preparing possible solutions.

  • *Activate the subconscious*

- Now that your main tasks are in focus and possible solutions are in the background, the **new, busy day** ahead of you no longer seems grey and cumbersome, but well-defined, **planned and altogether more accessible**.

  • *Structure of a complex working day*

67

MANAGING YOUR TIME

- **Less distraction and 'procrastinitis'**

- It will be **more difficult** for less important matters to **distract** you. Until now, because of your preoccupation with minor matters, you have repeatedly – and willingly – put off important tasks until you could only fit them in by working overtime – often with unsatisfactory results.

Don't let yourself be distracted by unimportant matters.

! **Remember:**
A busy day does not necessarily mean **stress**.

On the contrary, **a difficult job well done** will bring satisfaction and even a **feeling of relaxation**.

Stress results from matters not dealt with and a bad conscience

To reiterate, **stress** does not come from the work we have tackled but rather from the work we have not got to grips with: what we are not in control of is in control of us! Stress is a **bad conscience**.

Consistency and self-discipline

Once again: **be and remain consistent** when working with written daily schedules and priorities. Initially, using a time planner requires a certain amount of **self-discipline**, as do all good intentions – but it is definitely worthwhile.

We hope that you will have **more time** and plenty of success!

TRY TO BE CONSISTENT

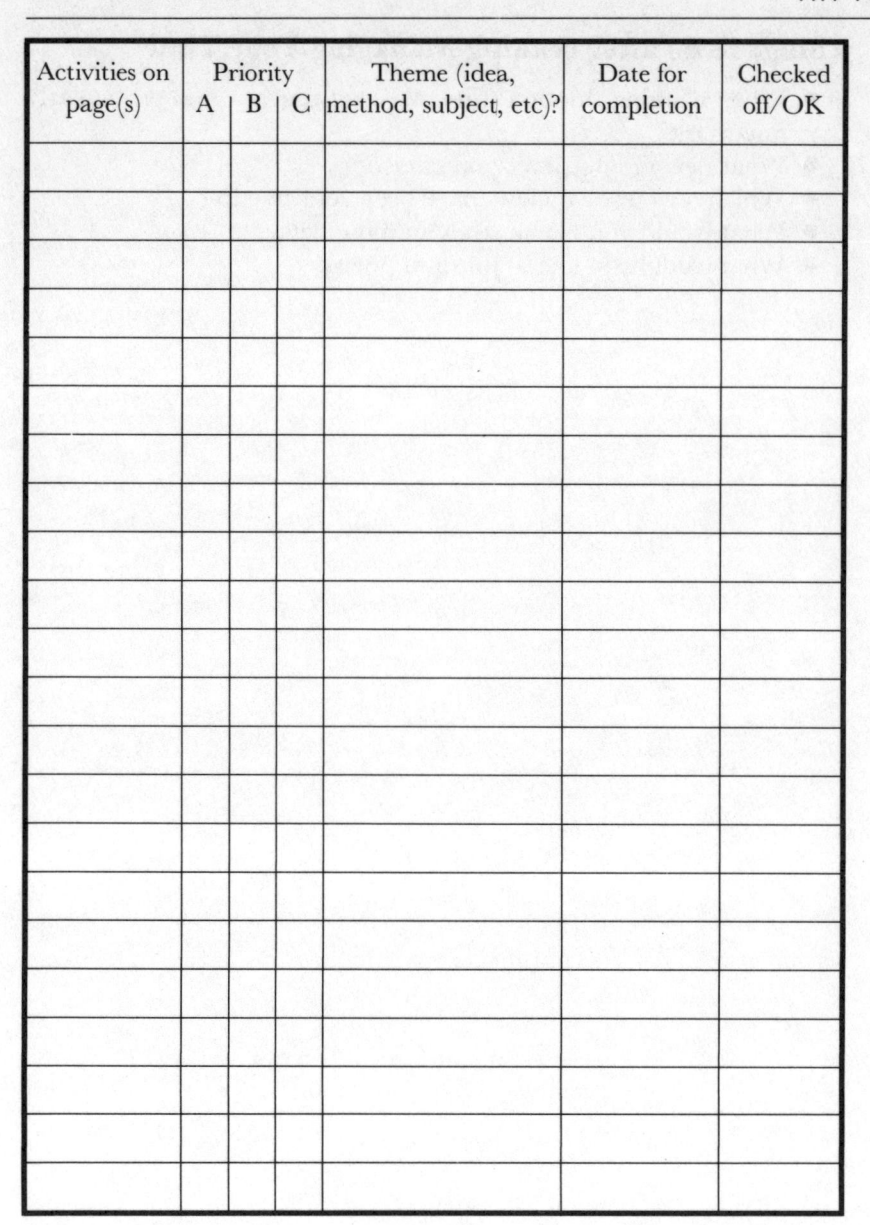

Activities on page(s)	Priority A	B	C	Theme (idea, method, subject, etc)?	Date for completion	Checked off/OK

Things to do after reading Managing Your Time

Put into daily practice

- When working through this text, what did you find particularly important?
- What new insights have you gained?
- Which of your own views have been confirmed?
- What would you like to study in more detail?
- What would you like to put into practice?

FURTHER READING FROM KOGAN PAGE

Don't Do. Delegate! The Secret Power of Successful Managers, James M Jenks and John M Kelly, 1986
Essential Management Checklists, Jeffrey P Davidson, 1987
A Handbook of Management Techniques, Michael Armstrong, 1986
How to Be an Even Better Manager, Michael Armstrong, 1988
How to Make Meetings Work, Malcolm Peel, 1988
Never Take No for an Answer, Samfrits Le Poole, 1987
The Practice of Successful Business Management, Kenneth Winckles, 1986
Profits from Improved Productivity, Fiona Halse and John Humphrey, 1988
Readymade Business Letters, Jim Dening, 1986
Winning Strategies for Managing People: A Task Directed Guide, Robert Irwin and Rita Wolenik, 1986

Better Management Skills

Effective Meeting Skills: How to Make Meetings More Productive, Marion E Haynes
Effective Performance Appraisals, Robert B Maddux
Effective Presentation Skills, Steve Mandel
The Fifty-Minute Supervisor: A Guide for the Newly Promoted, Elwood N Chapman
How to Develop a Positive Attitude, Elwood N Chapman
How to Motivate People, Twyla Dell
Make Every Minute Count: How to Manage Your Time Effectively, Marion E Haynes
Successful Negotiation, Robert B Maddux
Team Building: An Exercise in Leadership, Robert B Maddux

MANAGING YOUR TIME

Daily Plan

Schedule	OK
8:	
9:	
10:	
11:	
12:	
1:	
2:	
3:	
4:	
5:	
6:	
7:	
8:	
9:	
10:	

Contact	OK

Activity

Statistics

Personal

WORK SHEETS

Notes		OK

MANAGING YOUR TIME

Activities Checklist

D = Delegated for Action

Date	Priority A|B|C|OK	Activity	Delegated to	D	Start Date	Due Date

TS-form 10424 / © Copyright 1981, 87 by Time/system® International A/S . Denmark . Time/Design™ U.S. and Canada . All rights reserved.

WORK SHEETS

Activities Checklist

D = Delegated for Action

Date	Priority A | B | C | OK	Activity	Delegated to	D	Start Date	Due Date

TS-form 10424 / © Copyright 1981, 87 by Time/system® International A/S . Denmark . Time/Design™ U.S. and Canada . All rights reserved.

MANAGING YOUR TIME

Daily Plan

WORK SHEETS

Notes		OK

MANAGING YOUR TIME

Activities Checklist

D = Delegated for Action

Date	Priority A B C OK	Activity	Delegated to D	Start Date	Due Date

?-form 10424 / © Copyright 1981, 87 by Time/system® International A/S . Denmark . Time/Design™ U.S. and Canada . All rights reserved.

WORK SHEETS

Activities Checklist

D = Delegated for Action

Date	Priority A | B | C | OK	Activity	Delegated to	D	Start Date	Due Date

TS-form 10424 / © Copyright 1981, 87 by Time/system® International A/S . Denmark . Time/Design™ U.S. and Canada . All rights reserved.

The Business Action Guides

Agreed! How to Make Your Management Communications Persuasive and Effective, Patrick Forsyth
Appraising Your Staff, Philip Moon
Basics of a Successful Business Strategy, Kerstin Friedrich and Lother J Seiwert
Budgeting: A Practical Guide for Better Business Planning, Terry Dickey
Business Start-ups for Professional Managers, Pat Richardson and Laurence Clarke
Direct Mail, Charles Mallory
Forming a Limited Company, 4th edition, Patricia Clayton
How to Improve Your Customer Service: An Action Plan for Managers, Steve Macaulay and Sarah Cook
How to Perfect Your Selling Skills, Pat Weymes
Managing Your Time, Lothar J Seiwert
Practical Financial Analysis, James O Gill
Practical Marketing: A Step-by-Step Guide to Effective Planning, David H Bangs
Quality at Work, Diane Bone and Rick Griggs
The Small Business Action Kit, 4th edn, John Rosthorn, Andrew Haldane, Edward Blackwell and John Wholey